nature told me a secret

POETRY & MUSINGS

Nature Told Me A Secret is a work of creative non-fiction. The collection of poems and musings contained within this book are not about a singular person, relationship, event, or experience. The writings are thematic in nature, inspired by varied individual and collective experiences, conversations and reflections spanning through childhood, young adulthood, and adulthood.

Copyright © Naomi Arnold 2025.

All rights reserved. Content from this book must not be reproduced, distributed or transmitted in any form or by any means without the prior written permission of the author, with the exception of brief quotations embedded in reviews or other non-commercial uses permitted by Australian copyright law.

The content within the book expresses the lived experience and personal reflections of the author. Any views, reflections or advice contained herein may not be suitable for your individual context. Consult with the relevant professional where appropriate.

Naomi Arnold (Author)
www.naomiarnold.com

Illustrations (including cover illustration)
by Nicola Newman:
www.nicolanewman.com

ISBN (paperback): 978-1-7635708-2-5
ISBN (e-book): 978-1-7635708-3-2

nature told me a secret

POETRY & MUSINGS

Naomi Arnold

newsletter

Sign up to Naomi's newsletter to be the first to receive book updates, excerpts and news: https://www.naomiarnold.com/subscribe.

Content Warning

Abuse, depression, anxiety and grief

If you feel you need immediate support,
please call the relevant support services in your
country (e.g., in Australia, you can call
the Beyond Blue Support Service on
1300 22 4636).

Dedication

This collection of writing
is for those
who love and care
for nature
almost as much
as nature
loves and cares
for us.

Acknowledgment

Nature Told Me A Secret was inspired by time spent hiking amongst the trees, mostly on the unceded land of the Yugambeh people. This poetry collection would not exist without the inspiration I received whilst walking amongst the national parks and nature reserves within this beautiful region.

I appreciate that the Yugambeh people were the first poets and storytellers in this region of which sovereignty was never ceded. I acknowledge and pay my respect to the Traditional Custodians of Yugambeh Country and their Elders past and present.

I have deep respect for the connection, care and custodianship the Yugembah people have for this land, of which was and forever will be Aboriginal land. As I live, walk, write, work, connect and heal here - may I always remember the history of, and be humbled by, this land.

Preface

*In nature,
we find expressions
of what we cannot articulate
in human words.*

The above quote is from my debut poetry collection, *You Will Find Your Way*. I would be outside hiking or riding my bike amongst the trees when a feeling would land on me - a knowing - an epiphany that I could not articulate with human words but could feel deep within my soul.

As I spent more time in nature, I would frequently pull out a notebook or phone to jot down ideas, affirmations, or poems that were inspired by my surroundings. Each time this happened, it felt like nature was telling me a secret - hence the name of this book.

I hope this poetry collection resonates with those who love spending time in nature, especially those who find nature helps them move through traumatic experiences, regulate their nervous system, and heal.

I also hope the poems encourage you to occasionally put your phone away, be present, and really listen when you are exploring outside. Who knows what secrets nature might share with you!

NAOMI

An Invitation

I invite you to share images of this book, and your own realisations whilst out exploring in nature, on social media using the hashtag **#NatureToldMeASecret**. This way, I can follow along, connect with you, and read what secrets nature shares with you too.

Contents

Summer.............................. 1

The Port.. 3
Invasive.. 4
Memories..................................... 5
The Storm..................................... 6
Gullies.. 7
Angel's Trumpet........................... 8
Safety... 11
Blisters... 16
Whirlwind..................................... 18
Lifeforce....................................... 20
Determination.............................. 22
Nature's Steps............................. 23
Seeds... 24
Shade... 26
Grevillea....................................... 27

Autumn............................... 29

Backburn..................................... 31
A Secret...................................... 32
Nature Told Me A Secret............... 34
The Lean..................................... 36
I Was Found................................ 37
Eucalyptus Tree........................... 38
Spider... 40
Sprouting Manure........................ 41
Understanding............................. 42
Lounging Kangaroos..................... 43
The Portal................................... 44
Living Artwork............................. 46
Collective Care............................. 47
Outside Noise.............................. 48
Deciduous................................... 49

Winter 51

    Some Days................................ 53
    Tonight...................................... 54
    Burrow...................................... 56
    Underground............................ 58
    Dreams...................................... 60
    Nature's Telepathy.................. 62
    Double Rainbow...................... 63
    Swaying Branches.................. 64
    Growth...................................... 65
    Impasse.................................... 66
    Moonbaking............................. 68
    Bottlebrush.............................. 69
    Dendrochronology.................. 70
    Beginnings.............................. 72
    Winter Sunset........................ 73

Spring.............................	**75**
New Path.............................	77
A Vision...............................	78
Puddles...............................	79
Beautiful..............................	80
Sunflower.............................	81
Breathe Again........................	82
Unusual Is Beautiful................	83
Sunset, Sunrise......................	84
Magpie................................	85
Anthesis..............................	86
Pop of Colour........................	87
Mushroom Friends..................	88
Rebirth................................	89
If the Trees Could See..............	90

You Will Find Your Way.......   **93**

Nature.. 95
Internal Gardens.......................... 96
Dormant... 98
The Vine... 99
Like The Rain................................ 100
Wildflowers................................... 101
Blossom.. 102
Beach Walk.................................... 103

About the author **113**

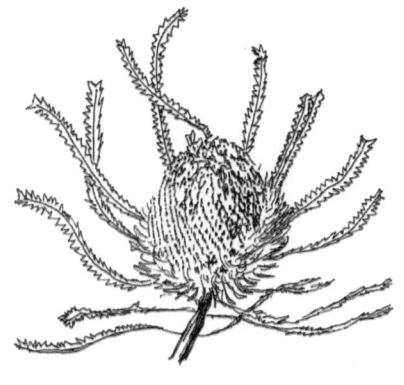

Summer

Prepared. Scorching. Thunderstorms. Resilience.

NAOMI ARNOLD

The Port

The beauty of the landscape
is interrupted by the touch of humankind
- the port, the concrete, the boats -
beautiful but ugly at the same time.

I try to visualise what it looked like
prior to my ancestors stepping to shore
- colonising, capitalising, destroying, denying -
I imagine it was indisputably beautiful before.

I pay my respects to the true custodians,
those who belong and tend to this land.
May I always remember the harm that was done
- past, present and future - on this sand.

Note: I wrote this poem after having dinner with friends by the water on Quandamooka, Turrbal and Yuggerra Country. I have thought these words many times whilst looking out at ports in other coastal townships, and on this day I decided to capture them and write them down.

NATURE TOLD ME A SECRET

Invasive

It begins with
    one little weed,
    one little thought,
and then it spreads,
    becomes out of control,
    taking over,
until you don't know
who you are anymore.

NAOMI ARNOLD

Memories

Lantana,
bracken fern,
bougainvillea,
snake weed.

Whenever I see them,
my mind flashes back.

Hours spent removing them.
A young, sensitive child.
No voice, no rights, no power.

An invasive pest
that must be controlled.

Automatic defense mechanisms.
The holder of a beauty unknown.
A complex story yet to be told.

Deep breaths -
I am that child no more.

The Storm

The storm came
without warning -
    hard,
    unforgiving,
    ferocious.

I didn't have time
to run for cover.

I was blown a mile away,
    left in the dirt,
    pelted with hail,
    thrashed with debris.

Then I was abandoned -
    left broken,
    forgotten,
    while you ran free.

Gullies

Gullies in nature
remind me of gullies in life.

Deep crevices,
open wounds,
scarred surfaces.

Challenging to reach.
Challenging to leave.

Water wildly flowing,
flushing out the debris.

Excruciating to navigate.
Heart-wrenchingly beautiful.

NATURE TOLD ME A SECRET

Angel's Trumpet

I sometimes think about
the danger of "the nice guy":

his charisma,
his humour,
his compassion,
his humility.

It lures me in,
it wraps around me,
it roots into my psyche.

I become concealed
within a canopy of illusion.

The outside world sees
what he wants them to see.

They think I am lucky.
They think I have "one of the good ones".
They think I am the problem.

NAOMI ARNOLD

But deep down I know -
I have become trapped
in the web of a covert abuser.

He reminds me of a beautiful plant -
 vibrant,
 luscious,
 fragrant,
 delightful.

But in reality,
it can be deadly.

Touch them,
ingest them,
and you will die -
 slowly,
 painfully,
 alone.

Beware:
the "nice guy" could be
an Angel's Trumpet.

NATURE TOLD ME A SECRET

Note: An Angel's Trumpet (Brugmansia) is an evergreen plant with beautiful trumpet shaped flowers found in many gardens. All parts of the plant, particularly the seeds and leaves, are toxic. The perfume, ingestion or rubbing your eyes after touching the plant can all cause severe symptoms and even death.[1]

[1] Queensland Poisons Information Centre. (2024, November). *Angel's trumpet (Botanical name: Brugmansia spp.).* Queensland Health.

NAOMI ARNOLD

Safety

Bush walking awakens so many
feelings, thoughts and memories -

a love for being in nature,
the awe of witnessing an evolving landscape,
a deep sense of wonder from observing
    the trees,
    the blossoms,
    the wildlife,

an overwhelming relief that sinks in
    as I do something for me,
    as I take a break from the chaos of life,
    as I pause from spending almost
    every waking moment focusing on others,

the calmness that washes over me
    as I feel the sun touch my skin,
    as the branches of trees sway gently,
    as my to-do list fades away,

NATURE TOLD ME A SECRET

a heightened sense of awareness and connection
with myself and who I am,
    with my emotions,
    with my thoughts,
    with my body,
    with my needs.

But in this state of heightened awareness,
I recognise these positive emotions
do not exist on their own.

Hovering behind them is
    complexity,
    caution,
    coexistence
    with an underlying anxiety.

Alongside these feelings of
relief, awe, and wonder,
there is an edge to me.

I'm still cautious,
aware of my surroundings,
cognisant of the fact that

NAOMI ARNOLD

as a femme-presenting person hiking alone,
    there is danger,
        there is risk.

Despite the relief,
there is caution.

Despite the calm,
there is nervousness.

Despite the awe and wonder,
there is a simmering anger
that he has taken even this
- my love for hiking -
from me.

Despite the love for what I see,
there is sadness in knowing
that even if it weren't for him,
it would never be fully safe for me to be here,
    to drop my armour,
    to release all my defenses,
    to just be.

NATURE TOLD ME A SECRET

How wonderful it must be
for those who can fully enjoy
    their hobbies,
    their psychological tools,
    the wonders of nature,

for those who can fully embrace
    the love,
    the awe and wonder,
    the relief,
    the calm,
    the self-awareness

without the haunting of an underlying
    caution,
    anxiety,
    stress,
    invisible load.

I feel resolve settle in.
I refuse to let them take this from me.

So despite the underlying heaviness,
I anchor in
    the relief,
    the calm,
    the beauty,
    the awe,
    the wonder,
    the love
of this place and of me.

I continue on.
I accept that this
is as free
as I'll ever be.

NATURE TOLD ME A SECRET

Blisters

I'm hobbling around
with blisters on my soles
because I opted for my Cons
when I should have chosen my Merrells.

My feet remind me
that I walked for miles,
and even though it was worth it
- for nature was a balm to my spirit -
next time,
I must care for
my poor, tired feet.

I realise this is on brand for me,
for it has been a life lesson
that self-care can hurt me.

Baths can lead to fainting,
exercise to injuries,
bed rest to back seizures,
massages to pain.

NAOMI ARNOLD

So as I hobble home,
with these excruciating blisters
on the bottom of my feet,
I am reminded of the steps
I missed today -

of the importance of preparation,
of the importance of slowing down,
but most of all,
that pre-care before self-care
is not a mere suggestion,
but a necessity.

NATURE TOLD ME A SECRET

Whirlwind

I watched a whirlwind today.
        It swirled and twirled,
it didn't discriminate,
        picking up leaves,
    small branches and debris.

        Then as it dissipated,
    I watched a piece of litter
fluttering and dancing,
    dipping and diving
across the sky like a bird
        amongst the raining leaves.

I realised in that moment
        I have been in a whirlwind.
    Life circumstances
spinning me around and around,
    taking complete control of my body,
throwing me in every direction.

NAOMI ARNOLD

And only now,
as these circumstances dissipate,
do I feel like that piece of litter
        fluttering around aimlessly,
knowing I will eventually find the earth,
    I will eventually feel grounded again.

            But for now,
    I give in,
        release my need for control,
and let the wind take me.

NATURE TOLD ME A SECRET

Lifeforce

The vine tightly loops
    around,
    around,
    around
the trunk,
    twisting,
    choking,
    scarring.

The vine feeds on the
    strength,
    resiliency,
    sustenance
of the tree
    clinging,
    tightening,
    climbing.

NAOMI ARNOLD

But the tree stands tall,
    reaching for the light,
    anchoring in the depths,
absorbing nutrients and energy -
    grounded,
    proud,
    growing,
an unshakable lifeforce.

I can be a tree.

NATURE TOLD ME A SECRET

Determination

When I'm out hiking
through the difficult terrain,
    my feet ache,
    my ankles wobble,
    my head pulses,
    my breath labours,
    my body simmers,
and yet I am determined.

I push through,
    and up,
    and around
the different surfaces.

I think of life curveballs:
    the heartache,
    the obstacles,
    the barriers,
    the evasive healing.

Just like this hike,
I will overcome them too.

NAOMI ARNOLD

Nature's Steps

As I hike amongst the trees,
pushing forward to reach the peak,
I notice that nature has created steps.
A way through and up the steep terrain,
    via rocks,
    gravel,
    concealed twists and turns,
    eroded valleys.
There is always a way.

Somewhere,
at the back of my mind,
I take note:
When life feels
    difficult,
    laboursome,
    exhausting,
I will find a way through.

Take a deep breath.
Search for nature's steps.

NATURE TOLD ME A SECRET

Seeds

You cup the seeds
of a dream in your hands.
You remind yourself to
handle them gently with care,
for you are holding
    new life,
    new possibilities,
    new futures.

You must offer them protection,
for they are
    delicate,
    precious,
    mortal.

They require the right
    conditions,
    environments,
    supports,
in order to
    germinate,
    transform,
    thrive.

NAOMI ARNOLD

But never forget,
these seeds are also
    strong,
    resilient,
    persistent.

They start small,
but can push through
    soil,
    concrete,
    obstacles.

They can survive
    harsh conditions,
    extreme temperatures,
    drought,
    flooding,
    fire.

With gentle resilience,
the seeds of your dream can
    grow,
    flourish,
    thrive.

NATURE TOLD ME A SECRET

Shade

In the sweltering hot sun,
I hiked up the hill that day,
decided to take a break,
pause to feel ease in the shade.

In that moment I realised,
I could take this lesson home -
release the need to push through,
seek out moments of relief on my own.

Grevillea

I am a grevillea -
bright and distinctive,
generous and giving,
resilient and adaptable,
creating beauty and possibility,
germinated by fire and smoke.
You will not destroy me.
I am a grevillea.

Autumn

Relief. Gentleness. Earthy. Transformation.

Backburn

To manage the trauma,
to handle the pain,
I ignited a back burn
    against my life circumstance,
    against the unhealthy relationships,
    against the persistent thoughts in my brain -
a controlled barrier
to slow and stop the wildfire
tearing through my life untamed,
to protect my heart and future,
so I could move forward,
heal, rebuild and reclaim.

NATURE TOLD ME A SECRET

A Secret

I have been keeping a secret.
I buried it so deep
that most days
it's even a secret from me.

I have been keeping a secret.
I buried it so deep
that even the trees
with the deepest roots
can barely touch it.

I have been keeping a secret.
When I'm amongst the trees -
I feel them reaching,
I know, they know.

I hear the secret whispering to me -
wanting to be heard,
wanting to see the light,
wanting to finally be free.

NAOMI ARNOLD

But as I emerge from the bushland,
unlock my front door,
return to my busy life,
the whispers are forgotten.

I have been keeping a secret.
I buried it so deep
that most days
it's even a secret from me.

Nature Told Me A Secret

Nature told me a secret.
When the swaying trees whispered,
I heard them say:

> be still,
> listen to yourself,
> you will know the way.

Nature told me a secret.
When the gentle wind touched my skin,
I heard it say:

> be gentle with yourself,
> your sensitivity is beautiful,
> it is here to stay.

Nature told me a secret.
When I stepped in the muddy puddle,
I heard it say:

> things will get messy,
> forge on through,
> I promise you will be okay.

NAOMI ARNOLD

Nature told me a secret.
When a spider web caught my face,
I heard it say:
                surprises will catch you off guard,
                    but your resilience
                      will hold you at bay.

Nature told me a secret.
When I spotted the most unusual tree,
I heard it say:
                        be yourself,
                    weird and quirky,
              your uniqueness on display.

Nature told me a secret.
When I went on my morning hike,
I heard it say:
                if you practise presence
                  and active listening,
        I'll share my secrets with you today.

NATURE TOLD ME A SECRET

The Lean

Like the tall grass
in the wetlands,
I stand with a lean now -
shaped by my environment,
working with the wind
rather than fighting against it.
Still flowering.
Still beautiful.
Still here.

I Was Found

(On the drive)
My mind took the lead.
I felt lost.
Outside of myself.

(On the trail)
Instantly grounded in my body.
I had arrived.
I was found.

Eucalyptus Tree

When I feel wobbly,
when my limbs tremble,
when my confidence sways,
when my energy goes away:
I close my eyes,
I take a breath,
I imagine I'm a eucalyptus tree.

Standing tall and strong,
feet anchored in the earth,
crown reaching for the sky,
    solid,
    dependable,
    hardy,
    adaptable.

Exuding earthiness,
    fresh,
    crisp,
    invigorating,
    confident.

NAOMI ARNOLD

I open my eyes.
I take a breath.
I imagine that eucalyptus tree
is in fact me.

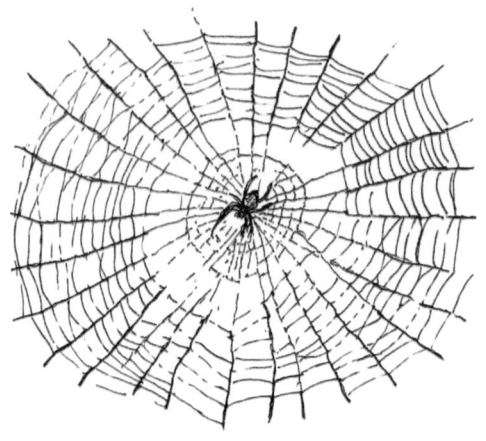

Spider

I almost walked into a web,
pausing just in time to see:
It was the home of a giant spider.
A reminder to be
    cautious,
    self-aware,
    present,
    respectful,
while exploring this place
that does not belong to me.

Sprouting Manure

On the trail today,
mind overwhelmed,
trauma rattling,
life seemingly exploding,
I glanced down at the earth.
I found a cute little seedling
sprouting from horse manure -
a sign from the universe,
a reminder of the new life,
the beauty and possibility
that can be born
from the shittiest of times.

Understanding

Nature -

You hear me,
I want to hear you.

You understand me,
I want to understand you.

You take care of me,
I want to take care of you.

You are part of me,
I am part of you.

Lounging Kangaroos

You inspire me -
>to lounge under the trees,
>to pause and appreciate the gentle breeze,
>to practise presence and simply be.

Thank you,
for unintentionally helping me see.

NATURE TOLD ME A SECRET

The Portal

On my walk today,
deep within the forest,
I came across a grand tree
with a little door at its base.

The door was slightly ajar,
revealing letters and toys inside.
I did not touch or pry,
for it was not my space.

I imagined the friendships
of those with belongings within,
the stories they may have shared,
bringing a wide smile to my face.

It felt like I'd entered a portal,
witnessed kids creating memories,
kids experiencing the joy of nature,
kids encountering the magic of this place.

Living Artwork

I saw a tree today,
white limbs branching,
shaped like a picture frame,
a beautiful landscape
set behind it
- living artwork -
ever changing,
depending on
    the season,
    day,
    hour,
    minute,
    and beholder.

Collective Care

We are processionary caterpillars,
connected and moving as one,
united against predators,
accumulating our energy,
nourishing each other,
stronger together,
no one left behind,
transformed we shall become.

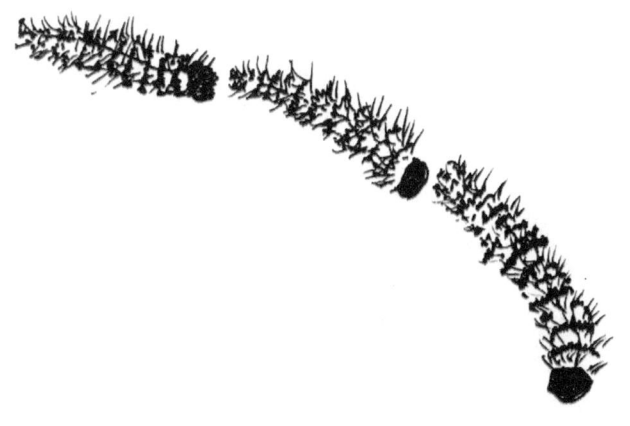

NATURE TOLD ME A SECRET

Outside Noise

I hike within the bushland,
eyes captivated by trees and sky,
a sense of relief only nature offers,
my stresses wave goodbye.

But even in the bush so deep,
I see the impact of humankind,
I hear the noise of the outside world,
thoughts begin to invade my mind.

Traffic purrs from a distant road,
abandoned litter leaves its mark,
regular planes fly overhead,
odd profanity carved into bark.

I feel a sense of awe and wonder
when nature demonstrates the possibility,
one can coexist with undesired interruptions,
whilst being rooted deeply in tranquility.

Deciduous

Today,
I drop my leaves,
shake away the insecurities,
strengthen my foundations,
stripped bare to the core of me.

Tomorrow,
I reveal all my colours and form,
stand confident within myself,
head held high,
blooming for the world to see.

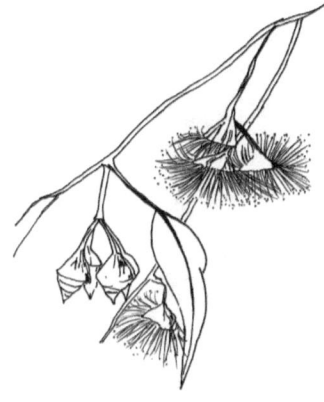

Winter

Dormancy. Shelter. Comfort. Contemplation.

Some Days

Be gentle with yourself.
Some days,
that same track
you hike every single day
is harder than other days.
Tomorrow may be easier.

Tonight

Tonight,
    I walk outside,
    look up at the sky,
    put a hand on my heart,
    release a breath with a sigh.

Tonight,
    you're on my mind,
    all you've been through,
    how lucky I am
    to have someone like you.

Tonight,
    I call to the moon,
    willing with all my might
    that things will get easier
    when you awake from this night.

Tonight,
> I quietly make a wish
> for only the stars to hear -
> may they share their blessings
> with you this year.

Tomorrow,
> when the new day breaks
> and you rise with the sun,
> I hope you feel a sense
> that a new chapter has begun.

NATURE TOLD ME A SECRET

Burrow

Burrow away
in that safe space -
hidden from predators,
protected from weather,
no invisible mask on your face.

Burrow away
in that dark space -
nervous system settling,
body resting,
away from the race.

Burrow away
in that quiet space -
replenish your strength,
build your capacity,
return to your base.

NAOMI ARNOLD

Burrow away
in your sheltered space -
gather your resources,
prepare as you need,
emerge at your own pace.

Underground

Withdraw, shutdown,
go underground.

Settle in your safe place.
Honour what you need.

Deep breath, in and out.
Stim, cry, shake it out.

Or curl up in a ball,
quiet and still as can be.

Discard any sense of urgency.
Remember the value of inactivity.

For you know
what nature knows -

the messages of sensitivity,
how best to build capacity.

For you know
what nature knows -

you are not lazy,
rest is growth,
dormancy is productivity.

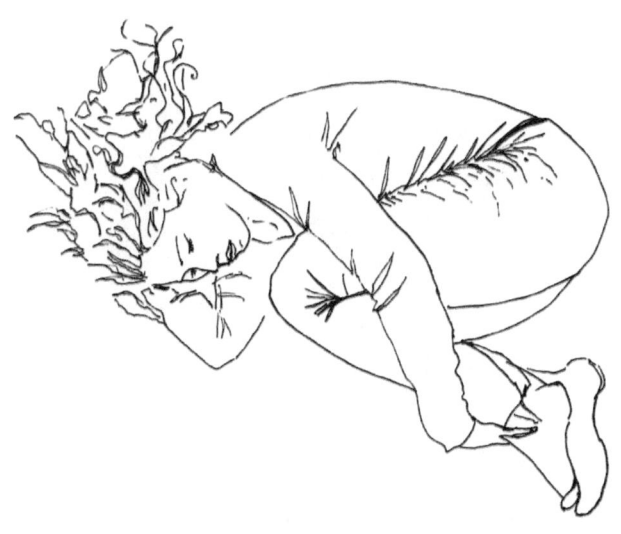

Dreams

As I plant the seeds,
I feel the wonder,
    the hope,
    the anticipation
of what and when
they might bloom.

As I plant the seeds,
I promise myself that
    I will water them,
    I will love on them.
    I will protect them.

As I plant the seeds,
I marvel at all the growth,
    the strengthening,
    the forming
that happens below the surface
- unseen and unwitnessed -
before they break through to the light
and begin to flourish and be seen.

As I dare myself to dream,
I too feel the wonder,
    the hope,
    the anticipation
of what and when
these dreams might
be fully realised.

As I dare myself to dream,
I promise myself that
    I will nourish them,
    I will love on them,
    I will protect them.

As I dare myself to dream,
I remind myself to marvel
at all the growth,
    the strengthening,
    the forming
that happens below the surface
- unseen and unwitnessed -
before these dreams break through to the light
and begin to flourish and be seen.

NATURE TOLD ME A SECRET

Nature's Telepathy

Nature is telepathic:
    it hears my thoughts,
    it practices active listening,
    it employs silence,
    it holds space,
    it is patient,
    it does not judge,
    it does not try to fix me,
    it simply witnesses,
    it mysteriously heals.

Nature teaches me to be telepathic:
my conscious mind listens
to my subconscious mind,
    I hear my thoughts,
    I practice active listening,
    I employ silence,
    I hold space,
    I aspire to be patient,
    I aspire to not judge,
    I aspire to not try to fix myself,
    I aspire to simply witness,
    I mysteriously heal.

NAOMI ARNOLD

Double Rainbow

Double rainbow:
one bold and vibrant,
the other not fully formed.

One who I aspire to be,
one who is currently me.

Someday I will show all that I am.

Someday that double rainbow
will reflect past and present me.

Swaying Branches

I observe the tree with curiosity -
branches swaying in the breeze,
the movement releasing tension,
shaking out the debris.

I find myself mimicking the motion -
gently swaying my hips,
taking rhythmic deep breaths,
as stress escapes through my lips.

Now when I feel a sense of overwhelm,
I remember to mimic the tree in the breeze -
bending and swaying with the wind,
allowing the motion to bring calm and ease.

Growth

A gentle reminder:

Dormancy is
an essential part
of growth.

Impasse

Some seasons,
some days,
the path is crossable,
the gully ranging from dry to wet.

>Without a thought,
>I pass through with ease,
>my mind focused on the trail ahead.

Some seasons,
some days,
the path is crossable,
the gully is now a flowing creek,
with exposed stepping stones.

>I pause and assess
>before carefully finding my way across,
>determined to follow the trail ahead.

NAOMI ARNOLD

Some seasons,
some days,
the path is seemingly uncrossable.
The gully is now flooding,
no longer safe to cross,

> I have a choice to make:
> *Do I accept the impasse?*
> *Do I turn around and go home?*
> *Do I risk attempting to pass?*
> *Do I search for a new way through?*

Only the season,
the day,
the path,
the mood,
will know.

NATURE TOLD ME A SECRET

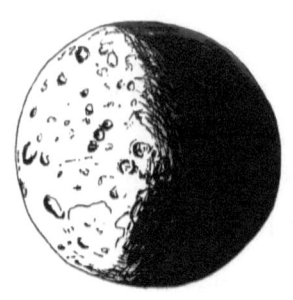

Moonbaking

Moonbaking under the stars,
bodies stretched out on the grass.

Dear friends, side by side -
hearts open, ready to confide.

Stories whispered under the night sky,
worries unburdened with an audible sigh.

Witnessed by the glow of the moon,
their giggles carry a faraway tune.

Together they enter a new day,
declaring dreams that are here to stay.

Note: This poem is for Paula, my dear friend and moonbaking buddy, for over 20 years.

NAOMI ARNOLD

Bottlebrush

I walk past the same bottlebrush tree every day.

Most of the time it is unremarkable,
blending in with the landscape,
quiet, ordinary,
just another tree.

But then suddenly it is blooming,
stunning and full of colour,
a hive of activity.
Bees buzzing,
butterflies fluttering.
A beauty impossible to ignore.

Then before I know it,
it blends back in again.
Seemingly inactive,
invisible once more.

Oh how I relate to that bottlebrush tree.

Dendrochronology

If I were a tree,
if you could see my growth rings,
oh what a story you would read.

Rings to show:
    age,
    history,
    environmental stress,
    pest damage,
    survival from adversity.

A hidden library of stories,
etched within my body.

Revealing:
    trauma,
    growth,
    strength,
    resilience,
    adaptation,
    beauty.

NAOMI ARNOLD

If I were a tree,
if you could see my growth rings,
oh what a story you would read.

Beginnings

Winter on Yugambeh land
will always be remembered
as the season and the place
when I broke free,
where I fully embraced me.

Surrounded by eucalyptus trees,
banksia blooming,
finches fluttering,
finally able to breathe.

Each year when the crisp air comes,
when pastel sunsets cling to the mountains,
I feel overwhelmed with gratitude,
a heightened sense of possibility.

Winter on Yugambeh land
will always be remembered
as the season and the place
when I broke free,
where I fully embraced me.

Winter Sunset

I am a winter sunset -
releasing the sharpness of the day,
embracing a sense of comfort and ease,
softening into the colours of me,
gently holding my hopes for tomorrow,
awakening a quiet confidence,
embodying my beauty -
I am a winter sunset.

Spring

Emergence. Awakening. Flourish. Possibility.

NAOMI ARNOLD

New Path

I look toward the new path,
it winds below the trees,
a track I am yet to follow,
the unknown causes unease.

I feel my heart rate quicken,
my mind begins to race,
intuition pulls me forward,
but hesitation slows my pace.

I glance toward the old path,
I know it inside out,
the ups, downs, twists, and turns,
a destination that causes doubt.

I feel my heart rate quicken,
my mind begins to race,
intuition pulls me forward,
determination quickens my pace.

NATURE TOLD ME A SECRET

A Vision

Deep in the bushland,
I peer between the trees,
eyes settling on a distant view,
a glorious pond beyond reach.

It feels like a glimpse of my future,
currently well beyond my grasp,
a promise of something remarkable,
if I'm patient and remain on this path.

The faraway pond offers a promise:
of the calm and stillness yet to come,
of a life full of beauty and wonder,
of realised dreams on the horizon.

Puddles

When I was a young adult,
rainy days would prompt me
to seek out puddles to jump in,
to squeal with delight and glee.

But now when I see a puddle,
I walk the long way around,
not wanting to get wet or dirty,
sensibly seeking dryer ground.

Today while I was hiking,
my dog splashed through the wet,
the puddle bringing him joy
while I avoided it with regret.

The moment brought a flashback
of a younger, more carefree me,
so I made a promise to myself
to jump in the next puddle I see.

Beautiful

It might seem strange,
but when I'm out
amongst the trees -
    old clothes,
    panting,
    out of breath,
    sweaty,
    flushed red -
I feel most myself,
    whole,
    beautiful,
    loved,
    seen,
surrounded by,
and full of,
    beauty,
    wonder,
    authenticity.

NAOMI ARNOLD

Sunflower

I am a quirky and confident sunflower,
standing lopsided alongside my friends.
Tall, proud, vibrant, happy.
You can't take this from me again.

NATURE TOLD ME A SECRET

Breathe Again

Fresh crisp air,
sunlight on my skin,
bird song all around,
eucalyptus in the wind.

A deep breath in.
A deep breath out.

In nature I discover,
I can breathe again.

Unusual Is Beautiful

What others find
unusual
about you,
I find
utterly
beautiful
and
awe-inspiring.

NATURE TOLD ME A SECRET

Sunset, Sunrise

Sunset -
a chapter closing,
a chance to let go,
the promise of a tomorrow.

Sunrise -
a chapter opening,
a fresh slate,
the hope of a new day.

Magpie

I am a magpie.
Vicious about protecting my young.
I will remember,
I will swoop,
if you ever do them wrong.

Anthesis

Each time I tried something new,
each time my confidence grew:

A flower opened in the barren field,
a heart awakened to possibility.

Until one day I looked around:
I was standing in a field of flowers.

Pop of Colour

I adore green,
for it is the colour of trees,
but you are the delightful pop of colour
that brings me joy in between.

Mushroom Friends

We are little mushrooms,
huddled together on the forest floor,
caring for and nourishing each other,
whispering and giggling together,
united for evermore.

Rebirth

The new me
was born here
amongst the trees
where there are
no witnesses
but nature and me.

If the Trees Could See

If the trees could see,
they would have witnessed
the broken me
hiking through the trees,
destroyed as can be.

If the trees could see,
they would have witnessed
the fighting me
hiking through the trees,
determined to survive and be free.

If the trees could see,
they would have witnessed
the healing me
hiking through the trees,
rebuilding confidence within me.

NAOMI ARNOLD

If the trees could see,
they would have witnessed
the weightless me
hiking through the trees,
finally able to breathe.

If the trees could see,
they would have witnessed
a transformed me
hiking through the trees,
finally safe to be me.

You will find your way

Please enjoy this bonus chapter containing a sample of nature-inspired poems from Naomi's debut poetry collection, *You Will Find Your Way*.

Nature

In nature,
we find expressions
of what we cannot articulate
with human words.

Internal Gardens

You have spent your lifetime
tending to the internal gardens of others.

You have consistently offered:
    protection,
    light,
    energy,
    sustenance,
    devotion.

It is time,
to entrust them with
tending to their own internal gardens.

It is time,
to offer yourself:
    protection,
    light,
    energy,
    sustenance,
    devotion.

NAOMI ARNOLD

It is time,
to wholeheartedly focus on
tending to your own internal garden.

YOU WILL FIND YOUR WAY

Dormant

Sometimes we are dormant:
    not visibly active,
    prioritising rest,
    conserving energy,
    building our root systems,
    replenishing strength,
    surviving adverse conditions.

Sometimes we are blooming:
    visibly active,
    vibrant,
    bright,
    loud,
    head held high,
    more obviously thriving.

Both are necessary.
Both are beautiful.

NAOMI ARNOLD

The Vine

Bending
    and twisting,

around your predefined structures,
following the rules for survival,
the guidelines for thriving.

Occasionally reaching,
        out into
              the empty spaces,
                  up tall
            in the sunlight,
        momentarily
    touching freedom.

But you always notice,
and swiftly take control,
wrapping me back around the structure,
back where you want me to be,
back to doing what I'm told.

Like The Rain

Like the rain
    takes the heaviness out of the humidity,
    washes away the debris,
    smothers the fire and heat,
    soaks deep into the soil,
    heals the scorched earth,
    and regenerates all things green,
feel your heart heal
and this new season begin.

Wildflowers

I aspire to be a wildflower,
            dancing tall and free,
not caring what people think,
not minding if they're called a weed,
            free,
            free,
            free as can be.

Blossom

You are allowed
to blossom
where it is
unexpected.

Beach Walk

Goodbye,
    blue horizon
    where the sea meets the sky,
    under the scorching sun
    where my dreams went to die.

Hello,
    toes grounded
    in the gritty sand below,
    a steady heartbeat resounded
    where new beginnings start to glow.

Naomi hopes you enjoyed this free sample of poetry from *You Will Find Your Way*.

A powerful collection of poetry for readers seeking comfort and inspiration after a toxic relationship.

In this raw and relatable debut, Australian poet Naomi Arnold provides solace, strength, and hope to those who have experienced betrayal, grief, or self-doubt.

Through honest verse and thoughtful prose, Naomi shows readers it is possible to find inner harmony, reclaim power, and live free from those who have harmed them.

PRAISE FROM READERS

"It felt like reading a music album and every poem is a song. And every song led to the next part of the story."

"Raw, honest, and full of emotion—sometimes painful, but always hopeful."

"Naomi's honest writing offers comfort and solidarity, highlighting themes of resilience and reclaiming power."

AVAILABLE NOW
https://www.naomiarnold.com/books.

An Ask

Did you enjoy reading *Nature Told Me A Secret*?

If so, please consider supporting Naomi by taking a moment to leave a review on Amazon and / or Goodreads.

Would you like to read more work by Naomi?

If so, you can find Naomi's other books via the following link or QR code:
https://www.naomiarnold.com/books.

newsletter

Sign up to Naomi's newsletter to be the first to receive book updates, excerpts and news: https://www.naomiarnold.com/subscribe.

Gentle Reminder

If you feel the content of this book has stirred up any big feelings and you need some support working through them, please reach out to the relevant support service in your country and/or the appropriate professional. In Australia, for example, you can start by calling Beyond Blue Support Service on 1300 22 4636.

About the author

Naomi Arnold (she/they) is a writer, researcher, award-winning life and business coach, and home educator. Naomi lives on the stolen land of the Yugambeh people in South East Queensland with their daughter and cheeky Cavoodle.

Naomi has a Master of Human Rights with Distinction, a Bachelor of Psychology with Honours, and a certified life coaching qualification. Naomi likes to draw on these topics in their writing, as well as her experience as an Autistic person with dynamic chronic illness.

Naomi's poetry collections include *You Will Find Your Way*, a powerful collection of poetry for readers seeking comfort and inspiration after a toxic relationship. Her latest poetry book, *Nature Told Me A Secret*, explores the lessons nature can offer on one's healing journey if we truly listen.

Readers have described Naomi's work as "strong, brutal and fearless", "deep and relatable", "raw and resonant", "unapologetic, engaging and inspiring", and "relatable, healing and hope-inspiring."

Learn more about Naomi via:
https://www.naomiarnold.com.

www.ingramcontent.com/pod-product-compliance
Lightning Source LLC
Chambersburg PA
CBHW020539080526
44583CB00013B/914